'TWIXT EARTH AND STARS ❧ ❧

POEMS

BY

MARGUERITE   RADCLYFFE - HALL

British Library Cataloguing-in-Publication Data
A catalogue record for this book is available from
the British Library

Radclyffe Hall

Marguerite Radclyffe Hall was born on 12th August 1880, in Bournemouth, England. Her parents separated when she was a baby and Hall was raised in a neglectful household with her mother and stepfather. She received her education at King's College London before moving to Germany to further her studies.

Hall's first novel *The Unlit Lamp* (1924) was a lengthy and grim tale that proved hard to sell. It was only published following the success of the much lighter social comedy *The Forge* (1924), which made the best-seller list of John O'London's Weekly. During the next two years she produced *A Saturday Life* (1925) and *Adam's Breed* (1926). The latter is a tale of a disenchanted head-waiter who decides to live as a hermit in a forest.. This work was well received and won both the Prix Femina Award and the James Tait Black Prize, a feat previously achieved only by E. M.

Forster's *A Passage to India* (1924).

Hall was a lesbian and had many lovers throughout her life. In 1907, she began a relationship with Mabel Batten, a well-known singer of lieder in Germany and twenty-four years her senior. Following the death of Batten's husband, the two of them moved in together and cohabited until Batten's death in 1916. The previous year, Hall had fallen for Batten's cousin Una Troubridge, a sculptor and wife of Vice-Admiral Ernest Troubridge. In 1917, Hall and Troubridge moved in together and remained a couple until Hall's death from colon cancer in 1943. Although the relationship spanned over twenty years, Hall was not a faithful partner and had many affairs of which Troubridge was painfully tolerant.

Hall is a key figure in lesbian literature for her novel *The Well of Loneliness* (1928). This is her only work with overt lesbian themes and tells the story of the life of a masculine lesbian named Stephen Gordon. This caused great controversy and was subject to an obscenity trial in Great Britain that resulted in an order for all copies to be destroyed. In the USA it was published only after a protracted legal battle. *The Well of Loneliness* ranked number seven on a list of the top 100 lesbian and gay novels compiled by The Publishing Triangle in 1999.

DEDICATED TO
MY INSPIRATION

I KNOW that through the waves of air,
Some part of all I feel for you,
Must surely travel swift and true,
Towards the heart for which I care
So dumbly, and before it lay
The words my lips shall never say.

IN A GARDEN

In the garden a thousand roses,
    A vine of jessamine flower,
Sweetpeas in coquettish poses,
    Sweetbrier with its fragrant dower.

There are hollyhocks tall and slender,
    And marigolds gay and fair,
And sunflowers in glowing splendour,
    Geraniums rich and rare;

And the wee, white, innocent daisy,
    Half hidden amid the lawn;
A bee grown drowsy and lazy—
    On honey he's drunk since dawn—

Is reposing with wings extended
    On some soft, passionate rose,
Aglow with a blush more splendid
    Than ever a fair cheek knows.

While a thrush, in the ivy swinging
    That clusters over the gate,

9

Athrob with the spring is singing,
  And ardently calls his mate.

For the spirit of all sweet odours
  The soul of a June unborn
Has hallowed my humble garden,
  And whispered to me since dawn.

And the flowers in a prayer of rapture,
  Bent low to that spell divine,
Are wafting their sweetest incense
  In clouds, at his sunlit shrine.

IF YOU WERE A ROSE AND I WERE THE SUN

(Song)

If you were a Rose and I were the Sun
  What then, little girl, what then?
I'd kiss you awake when day had begun,
  My sweet little girl, what then?
I'd waken you out of your valley of dreams
And open your heart with my passionate beams,
'Till you lifted your face to my ruddiest gleams,
  My own little girl, yes then.

If you were the Earth and I were the Dew,
  What then, little girl, what then?
Why surely the thing all lovers would do,
  My sweet little girl, what then?
I'd steal through the twilight, o'er valley and lea,
And flood you with kisses, both tender and free
Till the soul in you throbbed with the love that's
      in me,
  My own little girl, yes then.

11

But I am a man and you are a maid,
   What then, little girl, what then?
You're cold in your pride, and I am afraid,
   My sweet little girl, what then?
If you cannot love me and I cannot die
There's nothing in life but the ghost of a sigh,
And the day growing dark 'neath a colourless sky;
   My own little girl, yes then.

DRIFTING

It is sweet to lie in a boat,
   And drift with the languid stream,
With body and soul afloat
   The lake of a perfect dream.

It is sweet in the afternoon,
   With just the breath of a breeze,
If the time be the month of June
   And the birds sing low in the trees.

And the mind has a pleasant thought,
   And the heart has a fond desire,
And the soul is a tissue wrought
   Of youth, and it's golden fire.

And the limbs are both clean and strong,
   And able to rest with joy,
And our time in the world is long,
   With nothing that can destroy

The rapture of God's green earth,
   The throb and the ecstasy
That springs into life with birth,
   And lives through eternity.

TO ——

DEAR heart! I was going away,
  Could you not have spared me an hour
Of all your bountiful day?
  No moment, no word, no flower
To keep; not even a tear?
My soul was so thirsty, dear!

LOVE TRIUMPHANT

Ere the first grief was born
Love was.
And after griefs are gone
Love still shall triumph on.
Ere the first grief was born
Love was.

In Eden grief became
Love's slave.
For in the dust and woe
Lost Adam still could know
Fond recompense, and so
Did grief become Love's slave.

MY ROSE

A Rose! but what can it say,
  So tender, and sweet, and dumb ;
What part of my love convey,
  What thrill of the joys to come ?

I send it, but how shall you,
  Dear heart, ever understand
That rapturous tear of dew,
  It drops on your strong white hand ?

Or know that my lips have pressed
  Those petals until they blush,
Or feel that my heart has blessed
  The flower that your touch may crush ?

IF ONLY

Oh ! if one could only learn not to care,
To be utterly indifferent storm or fair ;
And to say there's always pain
With the joy, I don't complain,
For the sunshine draws the rain
      Everywhere.

Oh ! if one could only learn not to feel ;
To be absolutely callous, false or real ;
And to let the world go by,
With a laugh to cap its sigh,
With a jest to meet its lie,
      Cold as steel.

CONFESSION

WITHIN the portals of thy shrine
Before thy presence, dearest mine,
I kneel, beseeching thee to bless
My penitence, while I confess,
And can a saint do any less?

If I have sinned as others do,
All human hearts the wide world through
Are erring things, and then with me
My greatest wrong was loving thee,
Wilt thou condemn my constancy?

Look down, dear heart, and let thine eyes
Commend my soul to Paradise.
He little sins, who sins in this
That to obtain eternal bliss
Seeks the communion of a kiss.

SUNLIGHT ON DISTANT HILLS

(LEDBURY)

BUT a moment since and the sun was shining
  Over the hills that I see from my room.
And now the rain and the mist come driving
  Out of the West, in a cloud of gloom.
Over the woods, and meadows, and gardens,
  Hurries the storm like the hand of Doom.

But a moment hence and the clouds shall vanish ;
  Breaking and drifting and all asunder.
And lo ! in their midst will the sky be lying
  Calm and blue with a peaceful wonder
Nothing may alter, though sorrow and tempest
  Torture the Earth, as she trembles under.

MY LOVE

My love is a bird with a broken wing,
  Alone in a stormy night ;
My love is a lark that forgets to sing
  And dies with the morning light.

My love is a rose that the wind has torn,
  And crushed with a breath of pain ;
My love is song with the sweetness gone,
  A tune with a lost refrain.

My love is a ghost that has missed its way,
  A spirit from Heaven cast ;
My love is a joy of a bygone day,
  The soul of a burning past.

A MEMORY

No, I have not forgotten you,
    Although I went my way
Unanswered, as you wished me to,
    With none to bid me stay.

For in my heart there is a space
    Whose door you closed to me,
Locked in the memory of your face;
    Then took away the key.

TO ——

WHAT you deny me, you gave;
  You cannot take it again
In life and after the grave
  There is something that even then,
Death will not kill or destroy,
  It is so with the hearts of men.

Even your pride cannot rob
  My life of its blessed past;
You cannot recall one throb,
  One glance of the many cast
From those dear, passionate eyes;
  These things will be mine to the last.

ON THE MOUNTAIN

BELOW and above, yes, over and under us,
  Swift clouds hover, and speed and fly;
Nothing we see that can hurt or sunder us
  Here in the arms of the circling sky.

Surely we two must belong to each other,
  Silently mated where none are nigh
Save God our Father, and Earth our Mother,
  And sweetest of all, dear,—You and I.

TO ——

WHEN she turns aside to pass us by,
  With a little smile or a glance only
We are all alone, my Heart and I,
  We are all alone, and very lonely.

THE PRAYER

THERE stood beside the road a shrine,
  In whose quaint, vaulted shadow smiled
With eyes of tenderness divine,
  The Blessed Virgin and Her Child.

And I, who wandered all alone,
  Along a rough and weary way,
Felt that a great desire had grown
  Within my heart, to kneel and pray.

But lo! my voice had lost the power
  To utter words so deep and sweet,
And so, I breathed them in a flower,
  And left it, at the Virgin's feet.

IF

If all the words you spoke, dear,
Were every one untrue,
There can be nothing good, dear,
In earth, or sun, or dew;
And all the world's a lie, dear,
    Because of you.

If all the smiles you gave, dear,
Were only to beguile,
Why then there's nothing sweet, dear,
In any human smile;
And what we deem most fair, dear,
    Is only vile.

If every kiss that lingered
Upon the lips you pressed,
Was but an empty token,
More fickle than the rest;
I wish that I had died, dear,
    For death were best.

A LAMENT

Like a song that is sung, like a tale that is told,
  The life in me hushes the voice of its gladness;
Youth walks by my side, but his hands have
      grown cold,
    And deep in his eyes lurks the shadow of
      sadness.

Alas! for the flowers that never come to me;
  Alas! for the morning again, now day closes;
The joy of a love is as nothing, for through me
  There passes the deep-wounding thorn of the
      roses.

27

TO ——

THE wind's on the hill,
The sun's on the lea,
The lark's on the wing
And the dawn's on the sea,
And the rapture that springeth of Love,
  is on me.

THOUGHTS

Ah! the kiss of the sweet night air,
And the still, deep eyes of the cloudy skies,
Grown dim with peace:
Peace, the angel of death, that is everywhere.

Ah! the bliss of the soul at rest,
And of eyes that weep growing calm in sleep,
Hushéd by night:
Night, the shadow of death, that in blessing is
    blessed.

SHIPS

Fᴀɪʀ ships, happy and free,
Smile on the lonely sea,
Only to fade again
Into the mist and rain.
　　Ah ! me.

Thus do bright hopes appear
On life's vast ocean drear;
Hopes that beguile the mind,
And passing leave behind
　　A tear.

THE DREAM-CHILD

THERE is a child who will come to me,
Often at dusk, when my mind is free.
She is the child that I used to be,
    When I was only nine.

Over her hair is a wreath of flowers,
Those are the thoughts of the golden hours
Spent in the glory of childhood's bowers,
    Fancy, those thoughts were mine!

Butterflies whiter than flakes of snow
Hover around her lips, and oh!
They are the prayers that I used to know,
    God may remember still.

God who they tell us will not forget
Even a penitent child's regret!
Now I am callous of prayers, and yet—
    Ah, how I hope that He will.

THE DAY

THE day walks over the mountains,
To the splash of a thousand fountains,
To the song of a million streams.
Her hair is unbound and flowing,
Her eyes are as bluebells growing
In a valley of shade and dreams.

Her breast, than the snow is whiter,
Her lips, than the poppies brighter,
Her limbs are as strong white fire.
Thus she comes from the sky above her
To the arms of the Earth her lover,
In a splendour of warm desire.

FROM MY SOUL

Oh! but to find expression for the thoughts,
So marvellous and yet so undefined,
That flow from out the palpitating soul
    To consecrate the mind,

Oh! but to have the gift to put in words,
That potent passion, that divine desire,
That thrills the aching spirit with unrest
    And sets the brain on fire.

Oh! God, but once to rise above the flesh,
To breathe our inmost thoughts in one vast sigh
Of rapture. Oh! to realise ourselves,
    And at that moment . . . die.

WE

We who are made
Brave yet afraid,
Happy yet sad,
Good and yet bad,
Sane and yet mad,
What can we do?

Turmoil and strife,
Passion and life,
Love and desire,
Can these inspire
Spiritual fire?
How can we live?

Stumbling feet,
Tasks incomplete,
Longings that kill
Even the will,
Left to fulfil,
How can we die?

34

Little have we
Bond and yet free,
Strong and yet weak,
Proud and yet meek,
Save but to seek
God in it all.

God with His hands
Holds all the lands;
Rules every sea,
Sets the winds free,
Counts every tree,
Makes every leaf.

Then shall we fear?
He placed us here.
If God commands
God understands,
Ponders, and plans;
Knowing it all.

TO SINGERS

Sing with your intellect and soul combined ;
  Not all technique, nor yet all wild emotion,
Thus shall you touch the heart and please the mind,
  Winning a real and merited devotion.

THE MAY TREE

A GARDEN in the month of May,
The fading of a golden day
　　Upon the tulip flowers.
An anthem sung by little birds,
The sigh more eloquent than words
　　Of earth to listening hours.

And shadows . . . like the fringe that lies
On cheek, at close of drowsy eyes,
　　And paths, grown damp with dew ;
And secret places, where to tread
Were to disturb the bridal bed
　　Of creatures born anew.

And fairer than each living thing
That stirs with longings of the Spring,
　　A May tree, bearing flower.
Like some young nymph the sunlight charms
She stretches forth her slender arms,
　　New decked with leafy dower.

While through her wondrous, living form
The sap of life leaps strong and warm,
  Awaking from repose
The folded buds to know the Spring,
It seems I almost hear them sing
  For rapture as it flows.

Ay! and it seems as though my heart
Strained upward, but to take some part
  In that sweet hymn of praise;
As though my pulses quicker beat,
To see perfection so complete
  Revealéd to my gaze.

As though the problem of unrest
Were solved at last, in this behest
  To silently fulfil;
And deeper still, my soul perceives
The mighty Presence that conceives
  Such beauty at Its will.

PURGATORY

SHE said, "I want to live no matter what
The penalty, give me on earth the lot
    I most desire.
Let me drink deep of love, of joy, of life.
Scatter the roses, let the wine run rife
Dear Gods above, and then let fall the knife
    I will expire."

The Gods smiled sadly, very well they knew
Her ardent spirit could ascend the blue,
    And force their will.
Such weak old Deities these latter days ·
Could but comply to her imperious ways.
With woeful doubts they showed the flowery maze
    Of rapturous ill.

And she was happy : with that hot content
That burns away the flesh, that ravishment
    Of youth grown bold.
Until one morn the roses of her bed
Were turned to nettles, all the joy was dead,
    The passion cold.

She cried, " Now let me die, to live a day
Were Purgatory.   See the awful way
    I gaze upon."
The Gods were silent; powerless to avert
The consequence, grown wearily inert.
    So—she lived on.

TO ——

THE sound of the waves is the sound of tears,
   And the wind that drifts on the sea
Is the restless ghost of the bygone years,
   With their pain and their ecstasy.

The far white ships with their shining sails
   Are the hopes of a faithful heart,
Sent forth to fight through the storm and gales,
   With never a guiding chart.

And what of the pilot who stands above
   And steadfastly holds the wheel?
Oh! he is the man who believed in love
   Before he forgot to feel.

A SPRING POSY

A SPRAY of blossoms, and as well
Some violets, gathered yesterday
From leafy wood and shaded dell,
Sweet children of a fruitful May;
Dear minstrels of that silent lay
More potent than an organ's swell.

And now they're withered! all the joy
Has gone for ever, and the scent;
Relentless fingers can alloy
So much of nature's sentiment,
So many strains of deep content,
It takes so little to destroy.

AWAKENING

To open both your drowsy eyes,
To stretch your limbs and realise
    That day is here.
To watch the dancing, shifting beam
Of sun, awake yet half in dream,
Uncertain if the fitful gleam
    Be far or near.

To turn with soft, contented sigh,
And through the window watch the sky,
    All opal blue.
To feel the air steal in the room,
Made fragrant by the soft perfume
Of lime-trees, when their scented bloom
    Is damp with dew.

To hear the rustling voice of leaves,
The chirp of birds beneath the eaves,
    But now awake.
The tiny hum of timid things
That fly with gauzy, fragile wings,
Where yet the dusk to daylight clings,
    When mornings break.

To feel the soul look forth and smile,
Contented with each fruitful mile
    That it beholds.
To hear the heart beat loud and strong,
In unison with Nature's song,
That echoes tremulous and long
    While dawn unfolds.

To know yourself a thing complete,
With strength of mind and limb replete,
    With vast desire;
A creature made to dominate
The lesser things of earth, a fate
On whom the universe must wait,
    With force entire.

And then to cry in deep delight
God made the world and made it right;
    Dear Heaven above!
Was ere completeness so complete,
Was ever sweetness half so sweet,
Was ever loving half so meet;
    Thank God for love.

SHE IS DEAD

WELL! She is dead and gone,
  God willed it so.
Died ere her child was born,
  Ever to know.

Dead! oh, how still and cold!
  Yet full of rest.
She was not very old
  Still, it was best.

Hush, chide her not, not now,
  Save by a tear,
Dropped on that marble brow
  So smooth and dear.

Pity her as she lies
  There all alone;
Tenderly close her eyes,
  Sorrowful grown.

Yes; she has sinned maybe,
  Willing to fall,
Yet now forgive . . . ah! see,
  Death atones all.

TO ——

Dear, if you were in this city,
In this misty, dreary city,
With its sombre walls and towers—
All its poorer streets and byways,
All its richer streets and highways,
All the buildings stern and old,
And the river deep and cold,
Would become as summer to me,
Decked with sweet, perfuming flowers.

THE WHOLE OF IT

A joy that passes, a pain that stays,
    Such is life.
A moment's rapture, then weary days,
    Years of strife,
    Such is life.

A kiss of passion, a sigh of pain,
    Such is love.
A flash of splendour, then night again,
    God above,
    Such is love !

A sudden blindness, a creeping fear,
    Such is death.
An awful vastness, an unknown sphere,
    Choking breath,
    And then . . . death.

A SONG

A CLOUD is over the sun,
   The wind is laden with rain,
A frost has smitten the flowers;
   The time of Winter is pain.

But kiss me and I shall live,
   The sun shall nourish the plain,
The dawn be happy with birds,
   And love bring Summer again.

IF LIKE THE BIRD

If like the bird who sits and swings
Upon a branch, and blithely sings,
I could but spread two faithful wings,

And by their aid could smoothly skim
The highest peaks, the summits dim,
Until I reached the sunlight's rim,

Would I not then in pity gaze
Upon the turmoil and the maze
Of earth, and all its foolish ways?

A FRAGMENT

CHANCE made me look at you,
  Chance was no friend !
Sight made me worship you,
  Time without end.

Had I been only blind
  What had I cared,
And thus, afflicted sore
  How much been spared !

AN EVEN PSALM

WITH silent feet all wet with dew,
   Comes evening full of soft repose.
To kiss the valley deep and blue,
   With wistful lips, and eyes that close.

Her breath is soft, and full of peace,
   Her arms outstretchéd to caress
Fling benedictions without cease,
   She seems a spirit borne to bless.

And as the evening to the earth,
   Came love to me, a boon most rare ;
Hushed every sorrow at its birth,
   And turned complaining into prayer.

A BUTTERFLY

A BUTTERFLY hovered over a flower,
    In a bower,
With the joy of life at his lips for an hour.
With the rose's petals against his wings,
And the rose's perfume that steals and clings
Touching every breath with a wondrous power.

Then the Night came on, and the wind blew cold
    O'er the wold.
The butterfly shivered, grown tired and old;
The rose closed her passionate eyes and slept,
While death to her lover in silence crept;
He died of a joy untold.

DISAPPOINTMENT

How little there is that e'er goes right
In this old world of ours.
Anticipation? a vague delight;
Reality? well, the rose with a blight,
The thorn that comes with the flowers.

TO THE SEA

What can I sing to thee
Oh! thrice-beloved sea?
What words can paint thy grace,
The beauty of thy face,
Enrapt with ecstasy?

Fling up thy foamy arms,
Laden with cooling balms,
And touch me where I stand
Here on the yearning land,
With soft embrace that calms.

I gaze into thine eyes,
Where mystic shadow lies,
And lovelights glow and gleam
Within their emerald beam,
And passion lives and dies—

Until my heart grows still
Beneath thy magic will,
And I can hear and see
Naught but thy song and thee,
That seems the world to fill.

54

Upon thy swelling breast
Restless and yet at rest,
My spirit floats and sings,
While Summer laughs and springs
From off thy snow-white crest.

Behold my hot desire
For thee to quench the fire,
With dewy kiss that slips
From thy divine, wet lips,
Making my joy entire.

Lift up thine endless song,
And echo it along
Until all space rejoice,
In thine enchanted voice,
That sounds so sweet and strong.

Until the rocks and beach
Break forth in answering speech,
And every listening shell
Some praise of thee can tell;
Some joy of thee can teach.

Oh, sea that knows no death !
Oh, life-inspiring breath !

The heart of me would praise
The glory of thy days,
Thine evenings, fathomless.

The soul in me would sing
To that eternal Spring
Beneath thy heaving breast,
Where lurk the depths of rest,
The end of everything.

AFTER ALL?

THE gladness and the pain,
The sunshine and the rain,
The laughter and the sigh,
They all must pass and die;
  And in the by-and-by,
Who'll care to question why?

YOU

You have my thoughts and know it not.
The livelong day I think of you,
The still, dark night I dream of you,
Each moment's life I live to you,
᾿   And yet you know it not.

You have my heart and know it not,
Its every beat is love for you,
Each sigh a drop of blood for you,
Its ceaseless ache regret for you,
    And yet you know it not.

You have my soul and know it not,
It makes you God and worships you,
Forgets its claim on Heaven for you,
Forsakes its hope of life for you,
    And yet—you know it not.

REMEMBER

·REMEMBER, sweet! some evening when you sit
With idle hands, and book but half read through;
When those dear eyes of yours find incomplete
The landscape deep in shade and wet with dew;
When that clear mind of yours goes wandering out
To seek contentment, ay, and finds no rest;
When those grave thoughts of yours are filled
     with doubt,
And vague mistrust of all the world deems best;
Remember!—for one hour we conquered fate;
Filled in the blanks and set the puzzle right;
We were complete, a glorious, living whole,
A perfect cadence of supreme delight—
I think eternity was ours that night.

AN ECHO

In passion's hour I met you,
And now that from my soul I'm old,
Whene'er I watch the pale young moon,
Or misty glow of sunset gold,
Some echo of the past comes back,
Like wild, sweet song o'er lonely track
Lest I should e'er forget you.

FLOWER LOVE

" Where is she ? " sighed the rose-trees,
The honeysuckle creepers,
The pansies, and the lilies,
   And the little hidden flowers.
" We are lonely here without her,
In the sunlight, in the twilight,
In the daytime, in the night-time,
   Through the solitary hours."

" I know not," said the young wind,
" Yet will I surely seek her,
And whisper low your message
   Oh faithful-hearted few.
For men may kiss in passing,
And the world forget its passion,
But the soil, remembers ever,
   And the love of flowers is true."

THE FOND LOVER

I am but little in your sight,
A passing thought, a fleeting light
   That gone, forgotten lies.
The humble pastime, that you chose
To honour, as you might a rose,
   O'er which you cast your eyes.

Were I some simple, lifeless thing,
A book you read, an oft-worn ring,
   A favourite flower you wear,
I might be close to you and know
The rapture and the living glow
   Of lips, and breast, and hair.

But as it is, the earth you press,
The clinging texture of your dress,
   The jewel on your hand
Know more of Heaven and joys therein
Than I, whose soul has never been
   Where it could understand.

ROSES FALL

ONE by one the roses' petals fall to earth;
Though God's sun is still above them,
And the ardent breezes love them
    They must die.
Ere their greatest joy is born,
Lo! they wither and are gone;
Like a rose my hope must perish
    In a sigh.

A FRAGMENT

IF you were just one street away,
    One only !
I know that in my heart I'd say
    I'm lonely.

But with the world between us two
    A-lying,
I hear my soul cry out, " For you
    I'm dying ! "

DISSATISFACTION

Our love is near akin unto regret;
We love, and are beloved again, and yet
There oft is something that we lack.
So Life is very near akin to Death,
We live and laugh awhile, yet with each breath
Something is passing, that will ne'er come back.

ONE EVENING

The damp, sweet smell of the earth after rain,
  A golden rift in the sky,
The deepening twilight, the purple plain,
    And you and I.

The strange, still hush of the slumbering world,
  The mist in the wood close by,
A deer that nibbles a leaf dew-pearled,
    And you and I.

The falling rain has left tremulous lakes
  Where the shattered branches lie;
The storm has bowed the tree till it breaks,
    And you and I !

Yet the green earth smiles through the tears she
    wept;
  With one long, rapturous sigh
The Noon in the arms of Night has crept,
    And you and I ?

TO ——

I THOUGHT that I might see you, sweet,
  That after all this weary year
By some good fortune we might meet,
  And kiss each other here.

I told my heart to bide awhile,
  And not to faint with vain regret;
I even forced my lips to smile,
  My conscience to forget.

I killed depression as it rose,
  And built new castles on the sand;
This was the place my fancy chose
  That I should hold your hand.

And I have held your hand, my dear,
  A second, daring not to press
Your finger-tips, in mortal fear
    To meet your eyes; and yet I bless
    That little moment none the less.

MY SOUL, THE DEATHLESS

Hush! my soul is singing;
Through the still night ringing
  Sounds its voice.
Till the dark in wonder
Seemeth cleft asunder,
  And the stars rejoice.

E'en the air is breathless,
For my soul, the deathless,
  Sings of thee.
Beats its wings of fire,
In the vast desire
  For eternity.

Lifts its eyes of splendour
Full of deep surrender
  For thy sake.
Bids me let it press thee
In its arms, and bless thee
  Till thy love awake.

WHAT AM I?

WHAT am I to presume to say
Were you good or bad,
Was I wrong or right?
After all life's only a day
And perhaps—a night.

What am I to set up for Judge?
Shall I wound myself
With a vain regret?
Our fleeting pleasure if Time begrudge
Can he not forget?

The thrill of it all is past we know,
Say we both were right,
And we both were wrong,
There's little enough joy here below,
And love's none too long.

WHAT A PITY!

WHAT a pity that all our wishes,
   And most of our prayers are vain ;
When we strive to recall a pleasure,
   Or crave to forget a pain.

When the motives we deemed sufficient,
   Seem paltry, and mean, and weak ;
And the goal we'd have lost our soul for,
   Is that which we least would seek.

And the pride of those vast ambitions,
   That rendered our hopes so great
Has become but the coal-black cinders,
   Consumed in the fire of fate.

What a pity ! that blind with folly,
   We fancied all incomplete
Every flower of the true contentment,
   That grew by our careless feet ;

Nor did pause in our path, to gather
   The fruits of a gracious Spring ;
Or to seek in our hearts the anthem
   We called on the world to sing.

Ah, well! maybe God will remember,
　　As payment of many debts,
The penance of sad non-attainments,
　　The sackcloth of vain regrets.

And perhaps the Recording Angel
　　May wipe out the faults of years
With the hem of His shining garment,
　　Grown damp with a sinner's tears.

SONG

Good-morning, sweet! a thousand little birds
    Their requiem to you sing;
And tender flowers, with soft, perfuming words
    Their greetings bring.

Good-morning, sweet! this faithful heart of mine
    Offers devotion vast as Heaven above,
Beneath thy window, worships at thy shrine;
    Good-morning, love.

Good-morning, sweet! the glory of the day
    Is naught compared to thee;
Come forth and smile, with rapture bright and gay,
    That I may see.

Good-morning, sweet! look up that I may live,
    Kiss me that I may taste of Heaven here,
The joys of Paradise are thine to give,
    Good-morning, dear!

TIREDNESS

It is weary, weary this waiting,
  For that which can never be.
It is dreary, dreary this mating,
  With tears and despondency.

And methinks if beneath the grasses,
  There was somewhere, both still and deep,
I would close my eyes to the morning,
  And thankfully fall asleep.

ON THE LAGOON

A GONDOLA, the still lagoon ;
    A Summer's night, an August moon :
The splash of oars, a distant song,
    A little sigh, and—was it wrong ?
A kiss, both passionate and long.

A MORNING ON COMO

A SYMPHONY in pink and blue,
  A rhapsody of sun and dew,
A virgin Venus born anew,
  Lay Como in the morning.

And—"Would to Heaven some Muse divine
  Could guide this erring pen of mine,"
I cried, "to paint such grace as thine,
  Sweet Como in the morning!"

IN ROME

DAYBREAK. The heavy rumble in the street
Of waggons, journeyed from the sun-baked plains;
A laugh, an oath, as chance acquaintance meet;
The bark of dogs, the crack of whip and reins;
And then, with booming of combined refrains,
The ringing, swinging, singing bells of Rome.

Sunset, and purple shadows o'er the dome
Of sky above St Peter's; and the square
As silent as a graveyard, and as dumb.
Within the church, a peasant deep in prayer;
And like a challenge through the languid air
The ringing, swinging, singing bells of Rome.

TO ——

THE day is warm and mellow,
The fields are gold and yellow,
And in the misty distance
The hills are purple blue.

The Spring is up and stirring,
The pheasant's wing is whirring,
And there is nothing lacking
In all the world, but you.

.

HOPES

Our hopes are like the mountains that arise,
And to our dim, imperfect, human eyes
Seem in their splendid height to touch the skies.

Yet when we've toiled up, many a weary day,
We find the summit, desolate and grey,
And lo! the Heavens, still smiling, far away.

A MEMORY

Ah, dear! how memory stirs,
  Of meadows and soft-voiced thrushes
Of winds that sang amid firs,
  Or piped on the cool, damp rushes.

Of twilights and early dawns,
  And times when the earth is fairest;
Of gardens with dewy lawns,
  And flowers when their scent is rarest.

Of noontide and humming bees,
  That gather the love of roses;
Of night-time and sighing trees,
  And clouds where the moon reposes.

And, dearest,—of just we two,
  Alone in this world of splendour,
Where everything lived for you,
  In glorious, sweet surrender.

THE RIVER

Oh, river! sweet river, how placidly you wander,
  Yet bearing on your bosom so many lovers'
    vows;
Cannot the throb of passion arouse one wave in
    answer,
  Or stir to sighing cadence your silent willow
    boughs?

Must always—for ever, your brow be smooth and
    tranquil,
  Though hearts may break in anguish, or burn
    with ecstasy?
Is there no secret message that may arouse your
    wonder
  At all this vast emotion that thrills Eternity?

Some day though, oh, river! you too shall feel
    the magic
  Of all your depths awakened, of every tide set
    free;
Remember us in that time, we loving ones who
    sought you,
  When you have left the meadows for the em-
    bracing sea!

TO ——

LET not the morning break ere I shall say
  "Thou art the Sun that brightens all the day,
Thou art the Rose that perfumes all the air,
  Thou art the Soul of all that is most fair."

Let not the evening fall ere I shall say
  "Thou art the Star that guides me on my way,
Thou art the Moon whose beams are everywhere,
  Thou art my rest, my blessing, and my prayer."

SHALL I COMPLAIN?

SHALL I complain because the rain
  Has spoiled the flowers?
Shall I despair because the air
  Is damp with showers?

Shall I forget, that even yet
  New buds will spring?
And shall I sigh while still there's by
  One bird to sing?

TO ——

But, let me tell you all I feel,
And then, if you must still deny
No tears shall dim my sight, no sigh
Shall pass my lips, I'll only kneel
Before you in the dust and say,
"Tread on me, as you go your way."

MISTRESS SPRING

(*Song*)

Sweet Mistress Spring, all decked in green,
　How fresh you look this morning;
'Tis sure a year since we have seen
　Such flowers your brow adorning.

And will you come and walk with me?
　I'll prove an ardent lover,
Beneath the boughs of some kind tree
　We'll seek convenient cover.

There will I praise with light refrain
　Your most enchanting weather,
While you shall make a daisy chain,
　To bind our hearts together.

WHAT'S WRONG?

THERE's something wrong with the world to-day,
  What can it be, what can it be?
The morn is at six, and the year's at May,
  So mayhap that something is wrong with me.
    But there's something wrong,
    With the joyous song
Of the thrush in the apple-tree.

There's something gone from my heart I trow!
  That then is why, that then is why
The flower seems dead on the orchard bough,
  And never a sunbeam is in the sky.
    There's something gone,
    And the light of the dawn
Is the dimmer when you're not by.

GENTLE DAME PRISCILLA

(*Song*)

GENTLE Dame Priscilla
At her wheel is singing,
Singing of her lover, very far away.
Would I were that lover,
From my hiding springing
I would stop her singing in my own fond way.

Gentle Dame Priscilla
At her wheel is spinning
Fancies of her lover, who has gone to sea.
Would I were that lover,
Honey-tongued and winning,
It were then no sinning though I kissed her free.

TO THE NIGHTINGALE

Oh Nightingale, has that pale star heard you
Sobbing your passion into a song?
Has she deigned to stoop from her throne of
    splendour,
Deigned to pity your life's surrender,
Deigned to throw you a beam-smile tender,
You who have waited and loved so long?

Oh Nightingale, is your wondrous music
Cleaving the depths of the dark apart,
Born of a hope that is wearily dying?
Is she ever and aye denying
That for which you are always sighing?
Do you sing with a broken heart?

A MORNING THOUGHT

Wind and mist of the upland places,
Thrill and hush of the cloud-swept spaces,
Glow of sky that the sun embraces,
    Over a world of dew.

Purple-dusk of the sweet Scotch heather,
Golden gorse, in the summer weather,
Hand in hand, you and I together,
    If it were only true !

TO-DAY

To-DAY is a bumper of golden wine,
   Drink deep, deep, deep!
While the earth is green, and the cup is thine,
For there cometh an hour when a man must weep,
And there cometh a time when a man must sleep,
   So drink deep, deep, deep.

LOVE'S COMMAND

Love lifted up his eyes to mine,
   And in their depth did I behold
A flame, so potent yet divine
   That all the world besides seemed cold.

"Dear love," I cried, "come enter in
   And warm my heart with living fire."
Love answered, " First cast out the sin
   And rid my dwelling of desire."

CHANCE MEETING

I LOOKED up! you were standing there close
    beside me,
And just for a second our glances met,
And lingered, and mingled, and mingled yet.

I went on: you had turned and the spell was
    broken.
My temples throbbed, and my hands were cold.
I was longing, hopeless, and almost old.

ITALIAN SPRING

It is the Spring !
And what could be
So sweet a thing
As early Spring
In Italy ?

To make the boon more wondrous rare
You've caught the sunlight in your hair,
And, happy slave, it dances there.

To steal the splendour from the skies,
You draw their colour to your eyes,
Like deep blue lakes of Paradise.

It is the Spring !
And what could be
So sweet a thing
As early Spring
In Italy,
And you with me !

TO ——

OH! the awful pity of it all,
That I ever learned to care for you,
That we ever chanced to meet at all,
Since we neither of us could be true.

THE DIRGE OF A LONELY GARDEN

"I am a garden, alone, alone!
  Oh little Swallow pity me.
Over my paths have the lichens grown,
  Oh little Swallow pity me.
Down by the river the reeds are dank,
Close to the portal the grass is rank;
Nettles take birth on the lily bank.
  Oh little Swallow pity me.

"Once in the earliest days She came,
  Oh little Swallow pity me,
Sowing the seeds of my after fame,
  Oh little Swallow pity me.
Beautiful hands she had, and lo!
All that they touched would thrill and grow
Up to the sun of her eyes, aglow,
  Oh little Swallow pity me.

"Beautiful feet she had, that fell
  Oh little Swallow pity me,
Like the caress of one loved well,
  Oh little Swallow pity me.

94

Over the lawn at the twilight hour
Sometimes she wandered to pluck a flower,
Sometimes she paused in the jasmine bower.
    Oh little Swallow pity me.

" Then she would speak to me, sweet my own !
    Oh little Swallow pity me,
Words from her heart to my heart alone,
    Oh little Swallow pity me.
Tender, and ardent, and secret things,
Sprang to her lips, as the water springs
Up from the earth where the blue mist clings.
    Oh little Swallow pity me.

" I am a garden grown desolate,
    Oh little Swallow pity me.
I of them all, will remember yet,
    Oh little Swallow pity me.
Summer may come and summer may go,
I of them all who have known her, know
Love cannot die, though the loved one go.
    Oh little Swallow pity me!"

RESIGNATION

I ASKED you for your love again,
And I presumed too much it seemed.
The happiness of which I dreamed
Was but a jest, to laugh at then?
A trifle, that your wanton eyes
Beheld, yet would not recognise.

" I will be just your friend," I said,
" 'Twere better thus to be content
Than everlasting banishment."
You scarcely paused to turn your head.
Not needed, I had ceased to be
A thing for your utility!

I went my way, as others do.
These are not days to rant, and weep.
What pain there was I buried deep,
Together with my thoughts of you ;
And in that grave they lie apart,
Unmourned, save by a breaking heart.

ACCUSATION

How dare you cease to be my friend !
You who have held my heart and mind
Within your hand, a spell combined
Of passion and the joys that rend
Cast over all that once was me,
I would not if I could, go free.
I tell you to the depth of Hell,
My spirit, following in your wake,
Shall suffer for its folly's sake
Those torments which are yours, and dwell
Beside you through Eternity.

A SEA CYCLE

I

In at your cabin window,
  Under the drifting sky,
Softly, and all on tiptoe
  Winds that are passing by
Steal with a tender longing,
  Pause, with a yearning sigh,
Kiss you—and then in rapture
  Folding their pinions die.

II

THERE is something divinely happy,
　And something divinely fair,
At work in the world this morning,
　Its spirit is everywhere.

I'm filled with a sense of youngness,
　My limbs are alive and strong,
My heart with a throb of gladness
　Re-echoes the Ocean's song.

The sun is a splendid halo,
　That sets on the brow of earth,
The wind is the flute of silver
　He tunes to his strains of mirth.

The waves are abrim with laughter,
　The ship is a soul set free ;
And out through this perfect weather
　You'll presently come to me.

III

I PLEDGED you in a cup of wine,
And every passion that was mine
I melted in that nectar rare,
To drink to you, I swear—I swear!

I pledged you in the cup of life,
Its inmost essence, hot and rife,
I caught from drops my heart bled there,
To drink to you, I swear—I swear !

IV

LISTEN, dear heart, awhile, till I repeat
In all my life, there never was so sweet
An hour as this; so perfectly complete,
So full of joy, so deep and so replete
With ardent things.   Alas ! that time is fleet.

V

GOOD-NIGHT ! until to-morrow, dear ;
You go to rest, and I still here
Will dream of all you do and say ;
Will contemplate, as lovers may,
Each thing you've touched, with eyes that find
Your form in all you leave behind.

Your presence, and the joy that fills
The heart and soul with countless thrills
Is still beside me, and the ship
Throbs out with every rise and dip
The words that uttered once shall be
My music through eternity.

VI

LET me forget the land,
  The turmoil and the strife
Of cities; let me stand
  Alone with you and life.

Encircled by the sky,
  Uplifted by the sea,
The world is you, and I,
  Then give yourself to me !

VII

Don't speak! a word would mar it all,
    Just put your hand in mine.
This silence seems of Heaven, to fall
    From thence, a thing Divine.

Be still! to move would seem profane,
    So magic is the night,
All hushed, yet throbbing with a vein
    Of passionate delight.

Look up! and let your gaze enfold
    My face that bends above,
And in my ardent eyes behold
    The ecstasy of love.

VIII

I TAKE my heart with trembling hands,
　Unworthy vassal though it be,
Sad wanderer in many lands,
　Such as it is I offer thee,
And will not even dare complain
Shouldst thou this sorry gift disdain.

Yet oh! be sure that every sigh,
　Each beat of anguish deep and sore,
Has grown a dagger thrust, which I
　Must bear for all that's gone before;
And bearing it will learn to know
The cleansing agony of woe.

And this remember, ere you turn
　Your head away in silent pride,
The soul is young that still can learn
　New truths that Love has simplified;
And being young may still attain
Perfection, through repentant pain.

Then stoop to pity; do not close
　The gate of Paradise and rest,
To one whose spirit seeks repose
　Within that haven of the blest;
But rather fling the portal wide
And draw the pilgrim safe inside.

IX

THE past is like an empty dream;
　The people in it are not real;
The joys and sorrows only seem
　As phantom hands I cannot feel.

I will not even count the hours,
　That lie between those yesterdays
And what my present life embowers,
　Of love and all its golden ways.

All that I am, my soul, my mind,
　And all I ever hope to be
I fling, with scarce a look behind
　Into this present ecstasy.

I have not even one regret
　To waste upon those lagging years,
Too colourless to feign forget,
　Too soulless for repentant tears.

No sigh, though life should end for me
　To-day; so potent is the bliss
Of love, I think eternity
　Is held embodied in a kiss.

X

If every rose that ever blew,
  All fragrant with the breath of Spring,
Were here, aglow with sun and dew,
  With ardent petals shimmering—
What would their beauty count to me,
Have I not lived to look on thee?

If every note of music born,
  Each wistful cadence low and sweet,
Were all combined from night till dawn
  To render melody complete—
Why should my throbbing sense rejoice
That once has listened to thy voice?

Nor do I think that Paradise
  Could dim with raptured awe my gaze,
Unfolding to my dazzled eyes—
  The marvel of untrodden ways;
For know I not of Heaven a part
Since I have found thy living heart?

XI

Oh, my beloved! though I live
A thousand years upon the earth,
And though each pleasure take its birth
From me; though it be mine to give all
Rapture, every thrill and joy
Known unto gods; though I destroy
All ills, and overcome e'en death
Within the vapour of a breath,
That from thy lips passed into mine,
Fire-tipped, of earth, yet all divine
Would be contained more ecstasy,
To chain the soul eternally
With fetters woven of thy kiss—
Than in Mahomet's realms of bliss—
Nay more—of Heaven I ask but this.

XII

Over the silent waters
  Flashes the beacon light,
Sharp as a strong, white dagger
  Cleaving the breast of Night.

Beacon of hope and safety!
  See, we are near the land,
Come and stand close beside me,
  Give me your dear, white hand.

Here in the wind and darkness,
  Under the sighing mast,
Let us forget the future
  Let us condone the past.

God in His high, blue Heaven,
  Counting the falling tears,
Grants us this fleeting present,
  Out of the endless years.

XIII

THE land! The land! it is the end
Of all my dreams; the sudden bend
Along the road, and face to face
I stand with some deserted place,
Where Death, and Darkness grow apace.

The land! The land! with beating heart
I am awake, alone, apart;
To gaze upon the nearing shore,
And know that all that's gone before
Means nothing to you any more.

The land! The land! Oh, blessed sea!
Lift up your arms and cover me;
One long caress upon your breast!
You know me, I have stood confessed
Before you, now I fain would rest.

XIV

Oh, Time! There's much I could forgive:
E'en though you told me that to live
Another hour it was denied,
I think I'd lay my life aside
With few regrets, and scarce a sigh,
It would not be so hard to die.

But like a thief steals in the night,
You robbed me; what was mine by right
Your ruthless hands have snatched away;
The passions that were yesterday
You've cankered with your deadly rust,
And turned a living heart to dust.

XV

Ah ! if but once again to hear
The song of waves against the keel!
The sound of winds upon the sea,
To watch the moonlight, and to feel
Your hand in mine ; to have you steal
More close, more close, till senses reel,
And all the deep, unfathomed bliss
Of Life and Death were in your kiss.

XVI

I HAVE striven for three whole years to forget ;
I have prayed, ay, grovelled to God ; and yet
At the glimpse of a pictured face, of a form
That suggested yours—like a blighting storm
The Past rose up, and in anguish cried,
·"Oh, fool! I live, it was You who died."

Lightning Source UK Ltd.
Milton Keynes UK
UKOW04f2249041217
313862UK00001B/87/P